BENJAMIN'S POETRY

BENJAMIN FICKINGER

LIGHT SWITCH
PRESS

Published by:
Light Switch Press
PO Box 272847
Fort Collins, CO 80527

Copyright © 2021
ISBN: 978-1-953284-42-6
Printed in the United States of America

MY PERSONAL MISSION STATEMENT

-To use my poetry as a tool to show others with mental health issues that they
are not alone.
-To encourage others
-To please God in all I do

A verse that helps me remember this is Ephesians 2:10
"For we are His workmanship created in Christ Jesus for good works which
God prepared beforehand that we should walk in them"

INTRODUCTION

These poems in this book are meant to help people who are going through rough patterns in their mental illness and to encourage them where needed with my faith. The compilation in this book is: a reflection of my own emotions and struggles with Mental Illness, some light- hearted material as well as works reflecting my walk with the Lord.

Like Paul in II Corinthians 12:7-9, I have prayed and prayed that God would take this from me.

"And lest I should be exalted above measure by the abundance of the revelations, a thorn in the flesh was given to me, a messenger of Satan to buffet me, lest I be exalted above measure. Concerning this thing I pleaded with the Lord three times that it might depart from me. And He said to me 'my grace is sufficient for you, for my strength is made perfect in weakness' Therefore most gladly I will rather boast in my infirmities that the Power of Christ may rest upon me."

Many of the poems in this book I have written, while in and out of many different hospitals.

I would like to acknowledge the many men and women: Doctors, Nurses, Psychiatric Technicians and Therapists who have helped me over the years. I would like to acknowledge my parents and my sister who have always stood by me. I also acknowledge all my friends and my children: Ben Jr., Amzi, Josiah, and Eloise. Last, I acknowledge God who, through Him alone, gave me the words in this book.

ANIMAL FRIENDS

More than just creatures
They are pets
They are our Friends
Cause they sense our emotions
More they just creatures
They provide things for us like:
Milk, wool, eggs
Sometimes other things like
Hearts, valves and things
Like that.

More than just creatures
They depend on us
And we on them.
Just animals?
No! they are our friends

2/2/13

GONE

In the matter
Of a blink of an eye
You can be gone
Leaving family and friends
Gone.

In the matter
Of a blink of an eye
You can be gone.
Put that gun to your head.
Gone.

In the matter
Of a blink of an eye
You can be gone.
Put that needle in your arm.
Gone.
Gone forever
In the blink of an eye.

SNOW

You can go sledding in it.
You can make snowmen with it.
Snow! It is fun.

You can go skiing in it.
You can make snowballs   with it.
Snow! It is fun.

You can make forts with it.
You could play croquet in it
But I would not suggest it.
Snow! It is fun.

2/3/13

NORTHERN LIGHTS

The dazzling Brilliance
As the lights dance across the sky
takes one's breath away.
Shekinah (Glory)

The Dazzling Brilliance,
The colors,
Their super
Blue's and Green's
And others too.
It takes one's breath away.
Shekinah (Glory)

The Dazzling Brilliance
As the lights dance across the sky.
Do you see it?
Shekinah (Glory)

2/4/13

JOY

More than just words,
Joy.
It comes from the heart,
Radiates from within.

Joy
Can change your life,
Make you feel again.
You will find your purpose
Once more.

More than just a word-
Joy.
Search for it.
You will find it.

2/5/13

CANDY

One day in Hershey
I felt free.
I looked up at the sky
And what did I see?
Clouds.

Clouds
Fluffy like
Cotton candy.
But you cannot eat them.
They are fun to look at
If you do not want the
Calories.

2/5/13

AWAKE OR ASLEEP

Am I awake?
Or
Am I asleep?

The visions play over and over
In my mind.
It is hard to decipher.

Am I awake?
Or
Am I asleep?

The voices I hear over and over,
It is hard to decipher,
Are they real?
Or
Are they fake?

Am I awake?
Or
Am I asleep?

2/6/13

DENALI

It's huge-
It's great-
Denali.

Just to be there
Lost in it all
Is where I want to be,
To hide from it all.

The majesty,
The snow-capped peaks,
The sun in its rising,
The sun in its setting,
Over the mount
Denali.

To see it from the sky
Takes one's breath away.
It's huge-
It's great-
Denali.

2/6/13

PRISON

"Do this" and "Do that"
"You are this "and "You are that"
And things like these
Are all I hear.
It is tormenting me
Like I am stuck in a prison
And cannot get out.

Where can I go?
What can I do?
I just want to escape
I just want to be free
I feel like I am stuck in a prison
And cannot get out.

2/6/13

WELCOME TO HEAVEN

"Welcome to Heaven"
The party I want to have-
Why not now?
Why do I have to wait?
I just want to be with Jesus

"Welcome to Heaven"
The words I long to hear
will make me happy
Just to be with Jesus.
Why not now?

Why do I have to wait?
I just want to be with Jesus.

2/6/13

GIFT

On birthday's
We get these things-
Gifts.
On Christmas, too.

Gifts.
We give them,
We get them.
Some make us happy,
Some do not.
These are gifts.

Gift
The greatest gift of all,
The one that matters most,
This gift is
Jesus

2/6/13

CONTENTMENT

Contentment is a
Peacefulness that is within us
When we know that
People have our back
And
Friends stick by us.

Contentment is a
Feeling that all will turn out well
No matter what
We are going through.

Contentment is a
Peacefulness that is with us
If we allow ourselves to feel it.
It will make us happy,
It will make us strong,
Cause we know
That everything will turn out well.

2/7/13

THE OCEAN

Blues and Greens-
The color of the calm ocean,
The fish swimming.
How vast!
How big!
The Ocean.

The swells,
The crashing
Sound of the angry ocean,
Still the fish swim untouched
By the anger around them.

The calm ocean
After the storm-
Beautiful and serene,
With Blues and Greens.
How vast!
How big!
The Ocean.

2/8/13

PEACE

The feeling
Deep within us
That everything will be ok,
The knowing
That Someone has your back.

The feeling
That everything will be ok,
The knowing
God is in control.

The feeling
Even in times of calamity
will make us stronger
In the end.
Things will turn out well.

2/8/13

HESITATION

Hesitation
Keeps us from trying,
Makes us scared of doing new things,
Freezes us,
Even though time still goes on.

Hesitation?
"Hesitationology"-
The study of hesitating-
It silences us,
Freezes us, to stop doing.

2/9/13

CRYING OUT

From the depths of my soul
I cry
Cause the voices
Seem unbearable!
What am I to do?

From the depths of my soul
I cry
"Free me
From the violence within!"
Cause it feels unbearable.
What am I to do?

From the depths of my soul
I cry out
"Can anybody hear?"
"Does anybody care?"

From the depths of my soul
I cry!
"The voices- they're unbearable."
What am I to do?

2/13/13

HAMBURGERS

Hamburgers, Hamburgers
Many of them-
Big Mac and Whopper
Are two,
But my favorite is
The "Baconater".

Hamburgers, Hamburgers
Many of them.
Cheeseburger is one,
There are many others.
Which is your favorite?

2/14/13

THE STORM

The storm clouds
Rolling in,
Chaos around me.
But I long for a peace
During the raging
Storm.
The torturous voices
Tell me bad things.
I want to be free!
I long to be free
During the raging
Storm.
The storm clouds
Rolling in,
Chaos around me,
The impulses,
The urges,
I long to be free
During the raging
Storm!

2/15/13

HAPPINESS

Happiness is
Seeing the cream
In the Whoopi pie.

Happiness is
Seeing the smiles on my kids
As they greet me.

Happiness is
Being with friends,
Walking and talking-
And spending time together

Happiness is
A feeling deep inside
That can outweigh
The sadness
And Make for a good future.

8/12

HOPE

A glimmer of hope
On a bleak day
Fired him up
And gave him a strength
A purpose
He had not felt for a while.

A glimmer of hope
Is all it takes
To fire us up,
Take one day at a time,
And never give up.

A glimmer of hope,
A longing,
A yearning,
Hope for a better tomorrow.
Hope for security.
A peace
During chaos.

2/17/13

THE JOURNEY

They pierced His side,
Bruised and crushed Him.
A crown of thorns
Placed upon His head-
This He went through for us.

They pierced His side,
Bruised and crushed Him,
Spit at Him,
Beat Him.
A sign placed above His head-
"This is Jesus- King of the Jews"

They pierced His side,
Bruised and crushed Him,
Laid Him in a tomb.
On the third day He rose!
This He did for us.

2/18/13

WHAT IF'S

The "What if's" in life
Keep bogging me down
Like an anchor on a ship.
What if I do this?
or
What if I had done that?

The "what if's" in life
Immobilize me.
Cannot move forward,
Cannot move back.
Stuck.
What if I had done this?
What if I had done that?

The what if's in life-
How can I move past them?
How can I move forward?

The what if's in life
Keep bogging me down
Like an anchor on a ship.
What if I had done this
Or what if I had done that?

2/19/13

THE OUTSIDER

He felt alone
Like no one understood.
They were inside him-
The people.
Yet
He felt like an outsider.

There were those
Around him
Who knew nothing of this.
So,
He felt like an outsider.

He felt alone,
He felt like an outsider.

2/23/13

CAT

Cat- animal
Or
A machine?

A cat can be good
If you are stuck in the snow
Or
Stuck in the mud.
You cannot pet them
Or
Give them food.

But,
The other cat-
Originally a kitten,
Is soft.
And they
Usually let you pet them.
They are cute
And
Cuddly, too.

2/26/13

MILK

Milk is good.
It makes me feel smooth.
Chocolate milk,
Strawberry, too.
They all are good.

Milk is good.
Can cause a word war
Though.
There are many varieties.
Buttermilk
Though,
Is my favorite
To have with
Whoopi pies, doughnuts and Klondike bars.
Yes, milk makes my way smooth.

3/1/13

SUMMER SUN

The sun,
The warmth,
Summer is near.
To the beaches we will go
Cause summertime is near.

Summer is near.
Ice cream we will have,
And lemonade too.

The sun,
The warmth,
Summer is near.

3/17/13

THE STATEMENT

He was timid.
But one day made
A bold action.
A decision one made with
A statement that sent
Shock waves through all
Who were there.

"I want to go home
To be with Jesus is
My plea"!

In a split second
that sound sent
Shivers through all.
That man met his
Maker that day.

3/29/13

THE FOG

The fog makes
It hard to see.
Don't know which way
To turn.
Don't know which way
To go.

The fog
Makes it hard to see.
The way could be straight,
The way could be winding.

The fog.
Being stuck,
Hard to make
Things clear.
It is hard to see.

4/1/13

THE BRIGHT LIGHT

The young man
Standing in the shadows
Came out into the light
And said
"Come to me."

I started on my way
To meet him
When he said "Stop."
He looked into my eyes
And with a twinkle
Said "Come the rest of the way."
So, I started again.

I reached the man
But to look at him
I could not
For he was too bright-
Like the sun.
I could not even look into his eyes
For in him there was no sin
I said. "Forgive me Lord."
And he said,
"I have already forgiven you".

2/25/24

THE RAINBOW

The rainbow
A sign,
A promise
From God
Never to flood
The earth again.

The rainbow
A sign,
A promise,
The calm after
The storm.
A rainbow

4/3/13

NOTHING

Do we really exist?
Nothingness-
What the world was
Before creation.

Nothingness-
The act of being
Nothing.
Empty and void.
Nothingness-
Do we really exist?

4/8/13

NEW BEGINNINGS

With new beginnings
The old die
And have gone away.
We have a new start.

With new beginnings
The old die-
Hopefully gone forever.
Sometimes they linger
And crush us like
A load.
But,
We must find a way
To go on
Cause we can have
A new start.

4/21/13

QUESTION

Thoughts to die or not to die
Is the question.
Sometimes the thoughts to die are stronger.
Sometimes the thoughts not to die
Are stronger.

Thoughts to die or not to die.
How do I get
Rid of the bad ones
And
Keep the good?

5/10/13

ATTACK

Attack one
Attack two
Attack three
All in a row.
Then
I will be here no more.

Attack one
Attack two
Attack three
I want to be free
From the pain within.

Attack one
Attack two
Attack three
Maybe now
I will have my
"Welcome to heaven" Party.

5/24/13

OUCH!

When you stub your toe
You cry out "ouch".
When you have a headache
You cry out "ouch".
It is best not to say "ouch"
When someone is tickling you.

When you are eating ice cream
And you get a brain freeze
You cry out "ouch".
When you break a leg
While riding a lawn tractor
You cry out "ouch".
But again
It is best not to say "ouch"
When someone is tickling you.

6/15/13

CHALICE

The old man
With trembling hands
Held out the chalice
And said
"Please Lord fill it up".
Then he
Heard the voice of the
Lord saying
"I am the wellspring of
Life,
I am all you ever need".

So,
If the Lord, then
Is all we will ever need
They why not live like it?
Halleluiah Lord!
Thank you!

5/14/13

DOG

The summer
Is hot and humid-
The dog days of summer
When we drink lemonade,
Iced tea and iced coffee.

Dog
It is a pet that people
Like.
They are loyal,
Can cheer you up
When you are sad.

Dog
what kind do you like?
My favorites
Are Siberian Husky
and Dalmatian.
How about you?

7/24/13

HEADACHE

Some people get headaches
When they think
Too much.
You can get a headache.

Some get headaches when
They need caffeine.
You can get a headache.

Sometimes I get a headache
From my children,
From the chaos within
And without.
You can get a headache.

7/25/13

INNOCENCE

Why did he do it?
Take advantage of me,
Took away my innocence
And
Left me with a pain
So deep?
How can I go on?

I feel like giving up
But that's the coward's way.
Whey can't God just take
Me in my sleep?
So fast, so painless.

Anything is better than
This pain.
Please God, take it away.
Take me away.

7/29/13

DESTROYED

Destroyed
In the matter
Of a minute-
My life.

Hung in the balance
This pain stings.
How can I go on?
How can I make it?
Sometimes I do not know
If I go forward
Or
If I go backward.

Hung in the balance-
Waiting for me
To give up, to just die
And not to live.

8/2/13

HELP ME

My mind hurts.
Help me!
Take me away from it all.
Help me!

I want to hide.
Help me!
I want to run away.
Help me!

This pain, this torture,
Help me!
Why did it happen to me?
Help me!

Am I some freak?
Help me!
Send someone to me.
Help me!

8/3/13

AN AWAKENING

What good am I to others
When am I just hurting inside?
An awakening-
I would be better off dead; I am just dead weight.

What good am I to others
When I just wear a mask
And
Be someone who I am not?
An awakening-
I would be better off dead; I am just dead weight.

What good am I to others
When I am just crawling around?
I am battered.
An awakening-
I would be better off dead; I am just dead weight.

8/6/13

SOMETIMES

Sometimes I feel better,
Sometimes I do not.

When I feel better
I walk,
I talk,
I write.
Sometimes I feel better.

When I do not feel good
I cut.
I feel like I want to die.
I isolate.
Sometimes I do not feel better.

Sometimes I feel better,
Sometimes I do not.
When I feel better
I read,
I pray,
I play cards.
Sometimes I feel better.

8/9/13

SUNDAY

Christ is risen!
What a glorious day!
Our sins are
Forgiven
If we trust
In the Lord.

Christ is risen!
A new day dawns!
Rise up and rejoice.
Our sins are
Forgiven.

8/12/13

PAIN

The pain in my mind
is so real.
It is so raw.
How can I move past it?

The triggers, the scenes
Play over and over.
They hurt so much.
How can I move past it?

The pain- It is so real.
The pain- it is so raw.
Why did it happen
To me?
How can I move past it?
How can I move forward?

The pain is so real.
The pain is so raw.
I want to heal.
Help me heal.

8/14/13

HOUSE, NOT A HOME

The place where I live
Seems to have
no room for people.
I try to talk
But they do not want to listen.

The place where I live
Seems to
not want to help.
If you are in need
They do not want to listen.

8/15/13

RESTLESS

Going and going
And never stopping,
"Restless".
That is my name.

Walking and pacing
Restlessness,
Never stopping.
That is my name

Knees bouncing, legs going,
"Restless",
Cannot stop.
That is my name.

Going and going
And never stopping.
"Restless ",
That is my name.

8/15/13

THE VOICES

Voices torment.
I want to die.
I want to give up.
They hurt my mind.

The voices torment!
Free me from
This pain.
I want to go home
To be with Jesus.

The voices torment!
Help me!

9/15/13

TREMBLING

They make me
Tremble-
The voices.

They chip away
My life
Till it is unrecognizable
Even by my
Family
And
Friends.

The voices-
They are leaving me for dead.
I feel like giving up.
What is the use?
To keep on going.

The voices make
Me tremble.

9/24/13

MARCHING

My life moves on-
Marching forward
During all
The chaos,
Are my kids.

My life marches
Forward,
Hearing the voices
Of my kids
On the phone,
Hearing them say
"I love you Daddy"
gives me
Hope
To keep moving on.
My life marches forward.

9/24/13

POEM TO THE VOICES

Get away!
Leave me alone!
You have hurt me way too much.
You have put things in my head.
You have made my mind hurt, too.

I hear you talking,
Feeding me lies,
Things I should do.
Leave me alone!
You have hurt me way too much.

Get away!
I want my life back.
I want to live,
To be happy,
To be strong.
You have done enough
Damage!
Leave me alone!

9/28/13

WORDS

The word he uttered was
"Please".
"Please let me die".
"Please free me from this
Torment. Please"!

The next word he uttered was
"Party".
"I want a
Welcome to Heaven
Party".

" Please" and "party"
In the same breath
meant
"Please, I want a welcome to heaven party"

9/28/13

DROWNING

Oh yes, he was swimming
In the ocean.
But in reality,
He was drowning in life.

Nowhere to turn,
Nowhere to hide.
Yes, he was drowning in life.

He lost his family,
He lost his house,
He lost his job.
Yes, he was drowning in life

Nowhere to turn,
Nowhere to hide.
He was drowning in life.

10/8/13

THE DREAM

In his dreams
He saw a vision.
He was a prince,
He was a king.
No,
He was a great man.

What made him great
Was not his stature,
But his heart of a servant.

You see, to be a great man
You first must be a servant.
When you do this, you will find yourself.
Who knows? You may find yourself
A prince,
A king,
No!
A great man.

Then he woke from his dream-
A boy with a dream-
A boy who would one day be
A great man.

10/8/13

TALE OF THE HAPLESS MAN"

The hapless man
Went on with his usual routine,
When one day
His fortune turned a new direction.

The hapless man's wife
Went out and bought a lottery ticket.
That is when his fortunes turned
A new direction.

The couple watched
The news that night.
When the drawing went on
They looked at their ticket.

In the minutes that followed
They heard the numbers.
They thought they heard wrong
But they checked their ticket.

The couple
Found they had won the lottery,
And the hapless man
Found luck that day.

10/13/13

TRUST

In whom do we trust?
Our founding fathers said
"In Gold we trust".
Not in something, but in God.

You see,
To put our trust in something
Is to believe that
It will not fail.

Therefore, to put our trust in God
Is to believe that He will not fail.
And God never fails
Never, ever.

So, in whom do we trust?
The answer my friends, is God.
"In God we put our trust".
"In God we trust".

10/15/13

CHANGE

Popping pills
It is an addiction for me.
Lost my family,
My job,
My house all because of this.
It is time to make a change.

Change can be good,
Change can be bad.
But this change can help me
To live a normal life.

It is time to make a change-
To work on myself,
To work on my spirit
Because people need me.
My kids,
My family,
My friends,
And my acquaintances, too.
It is time to make a change.

10/15/13

REALIZATION

The realization hit him
That even though one day he would taste freedom
He would still give up.
He would have his "Welcome to Heaven" party.

The realization hit him-
There were none who understood him.
One day he would have his
"Welcome to Heaven" Party.
He would still give up.

The realization hit him-
Sure, he had kids he loved,
They were not enough to stop him.
One day he would have his
"Welcome to Heaven" Party.

10/16/13

DESTINY

Destiny
Wouldn't it be great if we had this or that?
Wouldn't it be great if we were this or that person?
What happens to us
Lies not in what others around us do
But,
What we ourselves do.

Destiny
Only you have the power to choose
What you do.
What you do will come to head in the future.

What is our destiny?
It is our fate.
Can be good,
Can be bad.
Only you have the power to do what you want.
Only you have the power to choose.

10/20/13

TEMPORARY

Why do I do it?
It is a temporary fix
To a long- term problem.
So why do I do it?

Why do it do it?
At first it releases me,
But the torment is still there-
The voices I hear

Why do I do it?
The voices get strong.
I just want to be free.
But it is a temporary fix
To a long-term problem.

Why do I do it?
I do it because it is easy-
So that I can escape
The voices,
The torment,
The pain
In my mind.

10/22/13

LOVE

Love is kind.
Love is forgiving.
Love is understanding.
And,
Love is candy.

True love is amazing.
Love is a warm bubble bath.
Love is heart, body and soul.
And,
Love is sweet.

Love is compassionate.
Love is respectful.
Love is caring.
And,
Love is sweet like candy.

10/24/13

FRIENDS

Friends are hard to come by.
Friends are rare,
But true friends stick by you
Through the thick and thin.

Through the thick and thin
Friends can be counted on-
Especially my friends.
They help me feel better
As we talk, laugh and spend time together.

Friends can be leaned on
When you have a bad day.
Friends can cheer you
When you are feeling blue.
My friends do this
And I try to, too.

Friends are rare,
But true friends stick by you
Through the thick and thin.

10/25/13

BIRTHDAY'S

Birthdays
With family and friends.
Birthdays mean
Presents, balloons, cake, pizza and cards-
Another year,
Aging year by year.

Birthdays are fun days
With family and friends.
Presents, balloons, cake, pizza and cards-
Another year,
Aging year by year.

Another year of
Birthdays,
Going to school.
Pastor? Or Missionary?
Maybe both.
Another year,
Aging year by year.

10/27/13

SHINING

The sun is shining
And so am I.
I feel super,
I feel happy
Even during showers.

The sun is shining.
It is warm
And
I feel super,
I feel happy
Even during Turbulence.

The sun is shining
And so am I.
I see through the
Tunnel,
I feel super,
I feel happy.
Yes,
The sun is shining.

2/16/14

NOISES AND VOICES

Noises are loud.
Sometimes noises are quiet.
The noises are the voices
In my head.
Go away
And leave me alone!
I want to be free,
I want to live free.
But there must be
A purpose-
To be used by God
To help others
When they are hurting.

Noises and voices.
I pray that
They may leave.
But I hear there is
A purpose-
For something good
To be used by God.

4/2/14

GUILT

Guilt is a weight.
A burden.
It is like an anchor
That pulls us
Under the Riptides.

Guilt is a weight.
Can ruin us,
Can kill us
If we do not get Rid of it.

Guilt is like
An anchor.
Can cause a lot of problems-
Pulls us under the riptides.

Send me a lifeline!
A buoy to help
Me get free from the guilt
Which is a weight.

4/14/14

A NEW YEAR

One day at a time
We are led by Jesus.
One day at a time
Our dreams are answered.
One day at a time
We can control our actions.

Our actions are controlled
By what we say and do.
One day at a time
We will spend eternity with Jesus.
One day at a time
We are comforted
By Jesus.
One day at a time
We are led by Jesus.

12/30/14

BLANK

What is there when
We feel lonely.
It is blank.

How can we feel better?
By feeling whole again,
Or better,
By the light that shines in the darkness-
a light that shines in the blackness.

What is there when
we feel lonely.
it is blank.
Pray for the light.
Pray for wholeness
Once again.

1/28/15

NO

When we try
Something
That is dangerous
We hear someone say
"No"!

Sometimes when we hear
"No"!
It is our conscience.

"No" is sometimes good
Because it keeps us safe
Rather than
Doing something
That is dangerous
For us.

So, we had better heed
The word
"No"!

1/29/15

ONE DAY AT A TIME

One day at a time
Is all we can do
To maintain ourselves
And not have too
Many highs
Or too many
Low's.

One day at a time
Is all we can do
To not hurt ourselves
But, to live life-
Our life,
To live life to its fullest.

One day at a time
Is all we can do.
Take one day at a time.
You deserve greatness.
Live life to its fullest.

1/29/15

COMMUNICATION

Communication
Is where the ball can
Be dropped.
I hear one thing
And
It happens.
But suddenly,
After a long time,
I hear something else.

Where did the ball get
Dropped?
I did one thing
Cause they said it was ok.
Why did it change?

I hurt deep within
So, all I can Do
Is use my coping
skills-
Singing, collages, word searches
And
Watching TV., reading books and writing poetry.

1/29/15

GOD'S GOODNESS

I hurt deep within.
But I read how
God is good.
I do not always
Believe it
Cause it seems as though
At times God
Is silent.

I hurt deep within.
I cannot
Get behind the funk.
God is good.
But I do not always
Believe it
Help me Lord
To see
Your goodness
In my life.

1/29/15

LASAGNA

Wow!
Lasagna is good
The tomato sauce,
The cheese
And
The noodles.

What kind do
You like?
Russian
That has vodka.
French
That uses French dressing.
Or
American
That uses "Prego"?

I like them all.
Which do you
Like?

1/30/15

HEAVY AND HURT

My heart is heavy.
My soul hurts.
During the chaos,
I know You are near.
This I read.

I cry out
For You,
But I have trouble
Hearing
Even when You speak
Loudly in my life.

My heart is heavy.
My soul hurts.
I know I need to:
Talk,
Write,
Watch TV,
Do word searches,
Sing, and make collages.

1/30/15

SALVATION IS AN APPOINTED TIME

The day of Salvation
I have read,
The appointed time
Too,
This is the day that
We should
Proclaim.

Our calling is
To share these things
So that others would
Know.

The day of Salvation
I have read,
The appointed time
Too.
Oh, what a day
To keep moving toward,
To see other's change.
Yes, Lord we thank you.

1/31/15

WALK IN THE LIGHT

Walk in the light
And
Walk not in the darkness,
I read.

We should rather then
Be the light
To the people
Who do not know,
The Light.

Walk in the light
And
Walk not in the darkness.
Help me Lord
To be light
To those who
Do not know you.

2/1/15

GOD'S GREATNESS

The greatness of God
The glory of God
I read,
The brightness-
We cannot see it.
We must close
Our eyes because
God's greatness
And
God's goodness
Are so awesome.
We must bow before Him,
For He alone is worth
It.
It is all we can do.

2/2/15

CARD'S

There are many ways
To play cards.
Rummy,
Poker,
Spades,
And others too.
Solitaire is another.

You can play
Solitaire by yourself.
But if you like
Playing with others,
Rummy,
Poker,
Spades,
And some others too.

I like playing
All of them
Except poker.
My favorite is
Rummy
Which is yours?

2/2/15

GRACE OF CHRIST JESUS

In the grace of Christ Jesus
We are to suffer hardships,
Teach others also,
I read.

As an athlete,
We are to be strong.
So be strong in Christ Jesus
And
Suffer hardships
As Christ Jesus did
On the cross.

He alone is our example.
So, we are to live this life.
Thank you, Jesus,
For what you did for us.

2/3/15

GOD'S BLESSING

God our Father blessed us.
He bought us
With
His blood-
For His inheritance.
This I read.

God our Father
Adopted us
To be His praise.
What a day it
Will be
When we will
Be with Him.
God our father
Bought us
With His blood.
So, let us live like this,
Because He paid
Our debt.
Thank You Lord,
For Your word.

2/4/15

TRUST

Trust in God
And pray without ceasing.
Ask in His name
And He will answer it.

Trust in God
And live in the land.
We will see His faithfulness
In our lives.

Trust in God
And give our lives to
Him.
And He will do it.

Trust in God
And dwell in God's land,
For He is our
God.
Thanks for being our God
And
Answering us.

2/5/15

GOD'S TIMING

We may not always
Believe that God's timing
Is when we want.
But God is always
Leading us
For His purpose.

Where we are is
God's timing-
Not ours,
It is in His choosing.
Therefore, we need to
Heed God's timing,
To be His hands and feet
To others.

2/6/15

GOD IS MY REFUGE

God is my hope.
He is my confidence.
He alone
Is worthy of
Our praise.

God is my refuge.
To Him we shall
Give our praise,
And to
Nobody else.

God is my hope.
To Him alone is
Our praise.
Every day
We shall praise.
We should live like this.
Help us to
Always
Live this
Every day.

2/7/15

OUR GOD

God, our God alone.
For us He died.
God our God alone.
He rose for us,
I have read.

God our God alone.
We must live
Like this,
And be His
Hands and feet.

God our God alone.
His grace He
Lavished on us
That we alone shall
Live like we
Are bought.
With His grace
Alone,
And not live
In sin
anymore.

2/8/15

WHAT A GOD

What a God we have!
Each of us is especially
Designed for greatness.

What a God we have!
Your work in us
Is not done.

What a God we have!
We are not alone
Because You gave us
Someone special
To spend our lives together...
The Holy Spirit.

What a God we have
We should praise Him
Forever.

2/9/15

OUR GOD IS AWESOME

Our God is awesome!
His glory, we will
Not see.
We will all bow down
To Him alone.

Our God is awesome!
We will
Serve Him
In all eternity
Just as we do
Now.

Our God is awesome!
He is worthy
Of
Our praise.
Hallelujah, Lord.
Help me to
Do so now.

2/10/15

NO MORE

"No more" is what
I say.
Friends I should be happy for
But feel
Jealous about.

I feel hurt.
I know I should bring it
To God,
But I feel like he will not answer
Or
If He does answer,
I may not like the
Results.

"No more" is what
I say.

2/10/15

ONE DAY AT A TIME

One day at a time.
Just hanging in there
And all will work out
Well.

I still feel hurt
because I keep it
All inside.
I pretend it does not touch me,
Like it does not hurt,
But it does.

Help me feel better.
Help the hurt
To go away.
Help me
Be happy for others.

2/10/15

MASK THE URGES

Behind this mask
I wear
The tears keep
Flowing.
My chest is heaving
And
My heart is pounding.

The urges are strong
For doing self- harm.
I know I should not
Because I have the skills
To help me get through this time,
These urges.

Behind this mask
Are two people.
They are like
Dr. Jekyll and Hyde.
The tears sting my
Eyes and face.
My chest is heaving
And
My heart is pounding.

2/10/15

PURPOSE

God has bought us,
From the dead,
Redeemed by His blood,
By the power of His name.

God is risen!
He calls us His own
And His work in us
Is not done.

God has bought us,
Gave us a calling
To reach others
For His own.

God is risen.
By His mercy
We are called
To be His hands and feet
To those who do not know Him.

WHAT

What is it that I ask myself?
When I want to do this
Or
When I want to do that?

What should I do?
When I am hurting?
I can bring it to God,
Talk to people,
And use other coping skills.

What is it I ask myself?
When the urge to hurt myself
Is strong?
I write poetry
And Use other coping skills too.

What should I do,
When I am crying out
But
It seems like
Its only in vain?

Just take one day at a time
And Hang in there.

2/11/15

ONE DAY

One day, when the Lord
Comes again,
We will be like we are in
His presence.
We will all bow down
To Him alone.

Blessed we will be
As we trust only
In the Lord.
He has promised
That we will be planted
And we will not be touched
By the evil in the world.
We will not be touched
And we will be safe in the
Lord's presence.

Blessed we will be,
As we behold the works of the Lord
In us all our days.
You have promised
And you will never fail.

2/12/15

DON'T GIVE UP

Like a tree
Planted by the river
Is my life
Which does not give up easily.
I keep on ticking
And take a licking.

During turmoil,
I press on.
I do not give up,
I just keep on moving
Which is all I can do.

Even when I am feeling bad
I look up at God,
And even though I do not see Him,
I do not know where He is leading,
but I just let Him carry me,
And trust Him completely.

2/12/15

OUR PRAYER

God, we pray that
You would teach us your
Ways
And that
We may obey
Your word.

God, we pray that
You would carry us even
When we cannot see
Where we are going.

No matter what people
Say and do to us,
You will not leave us.
Even when we may stray from You
You are always there
To pick us up.
Help us to follow you
All the days of our lives.

2/13/15

LIFE

God has promised that
He will be with us forever.
He has bought us
And given us a new life.

God is with us always.
He has promised
That when we give ourselves
To him
And Leave our sins,
Then He will give us a new life in Him.

Like a rock that cannot
Be moved
Is like God's love for us.
And,
We will not be moved.
This rock is like our lives
And
Shows us God's love,
He gave us a rock,
A shelter
For us to go to.

2/14/15

REJOICE

Lord you are holy.
You deserve our praise to You
Even though others may not.

We will worship You alone
With all our hearts,
Soul
And
Mind.
What a day that will be,
When we will be with you in Your presence,
With you forever!

In order to show your love,
We must love ourselves first
As well as others.
Otherwise how can we
Worship our God?

2/14/15

MY CALLING

It came to me one day
That one time I really
Wanted to be with Jesus
On my timing-
Right away.

But now I say I know that I should not
Rush the timing.
I can make it,
I can talk to people,
And use my other coping skills, too.

I have friends who care about
Me,
Who stand by me through
The thick and the thin.

Until the day comes
I will spend my time being
Committed to God
And
Doing His calling in my life.
You have reignited in me the desire
to reach others
For you thank you for my calling.

2/14/15

FOLLOWING GOD

Somewhere along the way
I slipped and lost my way.
Recently though,
In my Bible reading
And
Spending time in prayer,
I have found my way again.

I want to serve God as a missionary.
But now, I feel called to be a pastor,
A shepherd of God's people.
But no matter the cost, I need to be pliable
And do what God wants me to do.

I am ready to follow God,
To be His hands and feet
To those who do not know Him.

Thank you for this Jesus.
Help me to always follow You
All the days of my life.

2/14/15

THE MOMENT

The moment etched
In his mind,
Burned with fire.
A new life-
A life following God,
The call from God.
And, when God spoke,
He followed the instructions
That God gave to him.

The moment etched
In my mind,
Burned with fire.
A fire to follow you to its fullness,
To follow You and no one else-
To serve You and no one else.

2/15/15

GOD OUR HEALER

Oh God, our lives are
In Your hands
To do with, what you want to do.
During sickness
You have the power to heal us.

God, your word is true.
You can do with us
Anything you want to do.

God if we believe-
Even though it may be hard,
If our trust in, You
Is strong
, Or If our trust is small
You will still work
Your way in us.

2/15/15

A NEW DAY

A new day has dawned-
To be safe,
To one day getting out of here,
Doing what You want me to do
To share you with others,
To pray for others
And Serve you.

A new day has dawned-
A new day to live my life
To its fullest,
To be there for my kids,
To be an example for my kids.

A new day has dawned-
To be safe,
To be a friend to others,
To hang in there for
My friends and family

2/16/15

GOD OUR TEACHER

God, you are our Teacher.
Show me your way,
Lead us in your way,
And we will follow You
All the days of our lives.

God, you are our Teacher.
Guide us and train us
To go your way
So that we may follow you.

God, you are our Teacher.
Help us to show your way's to others
And When you speak, help us
To speak as you want-
Not Our way.

God, you are our Teacher.
We praise you
And Only you.
We will continue to
Praise you in this life
As well as in you

2/16/15

GOD'S GOODNESS

I hurt deep within, but I read how God is good
I do not always believe it because it feels at times
That God is silent
I hurt deep within and cannot get behind the funk
God is good though I do not always believe it
Help me Lord to see your goodness in my life.

1/29/15

SALVATION'S APPOINTED TIME

The day of salvation, I have read
The appointed time, too
This is the day that we should proclaim
Our calling is to share these things
So that others should know
The day of salvation, I have read
The appointed time, too
Oh, what a day to keep moving on
To see others change
For this, Lord, we thank you

1/31/15

WALK IN THE LIGHT

Walk in the light
and walk not in darkness, I read
We should rather, then, shine the light
For people who do not see the light
Walk in the light and not in darkness
Help me Lord to be a light
To those who do not know You.

2/1/15

GOD'S GREATNESS

The greatness of God, the glory of God, I read
The brightness we cannot feel it
We must close our eyes
Because of God's greatness and God's goodness
We must bow before Him
For He alone is worthy
It is all we can do

2/2/15

GRACE OF CHRIST JESUS

In the grace of Christ Jesus, we are
To suffer hardships
Teach others also, I read
As an athlete, we are to be strong
Strong in Christ Jesus
And to suffer hardships as
Christ Jesus did on the cross
He alone is the example
So, we are to live this
Thank you, Jesus, for what You did for us

2/3/15

GOD'S BLESSING

God, our Father blessed us
He bought us with his blood
As His inheritance, this I read
God our Father adopted us
To be His for his glory
What a day that will be
When we will be with Him
God, our Father bought us with his blood
He paid our debt
Thank you, Father, for your word

2/4/15

TRUST

Trust in God and pray without ceasing
Ask in His name and He will answer us
Trust in God and live in the land
We will see his faithfulness in our life
If we trust in God, give our lives to Him
And ask of him and He will do it.
Trust in God, dwell in God's land
For He is our God.
Thanks for being our God
And answering us

2/5/15

GOD'S TIMING

We may not always believe that
God's timing is what we want
But God is always leading us
For his purpose
While we are in God's timing
And not ours, it is his choosing
Therefore, we need to heed
God's timing to be his hands and feet

2/6/15

GOD IS MY REFUGE

God is my refuge, God is my hope
He is my confidence. He alone
Is worthy of my praise
God is my refuge. He alone must
Be praised, and no one else
God is my hope. He alone is our praise
Every day we should praise.
We should live this every day
Help us Lord to live this each day.

2/7/15

OUR GOD

God, our God alone, for He died
God, our God alone, He rose for us
God, our God alone. We must live for this
And be his hands and feet
God, our God alone, his grace
He lavished on us
We alone shall live as we were bought with his grace
And not live in sin anymore.

2/8/15

WHAT A GOD

What a God we have
Each one especially designed for greatness
What a God we have
Your work in us is not done
What a God we have
We are not alone for you have
Given us someone special to spend
Our lives together
What a God we have
We should praise Him forever

2/9/15

PURPOSE 2/11

God has brought us from the dead
Redeemed us with his blood
By the power of his name
God has risen and calls us his own
His work in us is not done.
God has given us a calling
To reach others for his own
God is risen. By his mercy
We are called to be his hands and feet
To those who do not know Him

2/11/15

ONE DAY

One day when the Lord comes
We will be in His presence
We will all bow down to him alone
Blessed we will be as we trust only in the Lord
He has promised that we will be planted
And that we will not be touched
By the evil in the world
We will not be touched, and we will be safe
In the Lord's presence
Blessed we will be as we behold
The works of the Lord through all our days
His promise will not fail

2/12/15

DO NOT GIVE UP

Like a tree planted by the river
Is my life which does not give up easily
I keep on kickin' and take a lickin'
During turmoil, I press on
And do not give up.
I just keep on moving.
This is all I can do
Even when I am feeling bad.
I look up to God
Even when I do not see Him
I do not know where He is leading me.
But I know I can trust Him
And just let Him carry me.
I must trust Him completely.

OUR PRAYER

God, we pray that You would
Teach us your ways, that we
may obey your Word.
God, we pray that You would
Carry us even when we cannot see
Where we are going.
No matter what people say
Or do to us, you will not leave us.
Even though we may stray from You
You are always there to pick us up.
Help us to follow You all the
Days of our lives

2/13/15

LIFE

God has promised that
He will be with us forever.
He has bought us and
Given us a new life.
God is with us always.
He has promised that
When we give ourselves to Him
Like a rock that cannot be moved
Is God's love for us.
This rock is God. He shows us
That He is a sheltering love for us.

2/14/15

REJOICE

Lord, you are holy
You deserve our praise to You
Even though others may not
We will worship You alone
With all our hearts, soul, and mind
What a day that will be
When we will be with You
In your presence- with you forever
In order to show your love
We must love ourselves first
Otherwise, how can we worship God?

2/14/15

MY CALLING

It came to me one day
That I really wanted to be with Jesus
In my timing- right away
I know that I should not rush the time
I can make it, I can talk with people
And do other coping skills, too
I have friends who care about me
Who stand by me through the thick and the thin?
Until one day, the time to be committed to God
And His calling in my life; to reach others for Him
Thank you for my calling.

2/14/15

FOLLOWING GOD

Somewhere along the way
I slipped and lost my way
Recently, though, in my Bible reading
And spending time in prayer
I have found my way again
I want to serve God as a missionary
I feel a call to be a pastor
A shepherd to God's people
But no matter the cost
I need to be pliable and
Do what God wants me to do
I am ready to follow God
To be His hands and feet
To those who do not know Him
Thank you for this, Jesus
Help me to always follow You
All the days of my life

2/14/15

THE MOMENT

The moment etched in his mind
Burned with fire
A new life, a life following God
The call from God, and when God spoke
He followed God's instructions
The moment etched in my mind
Burned with fire- a fire to follow You
A fire to live for You in fullness
To follow You and no one else
To serve You and no one else

2/15/15

THE HEALER 2/15

Oh God, our lives are in your hands
To do with what you want to do
During sickness
You have the power to heal us
God, your word is true
You can do with us anything you want
God, if we believe
even if trusting Him is hard
For trusting Him is strong even
If our faith in Him is small
God will always work His way in us

2/15/15

A NEW DAY

A new day has dawned to be safe
Today, getting out of here
Doing what You want me to do
To share You with others
A new day has dawned in my life
To the fullness, to be safe,
To be there for my kids
To be an example for my kids
A new day has dawned to be safe
To be a friend to others
To hang in there for my friends

2/16/15

GOD, OUR TEACHER 2/16

God, You, are our Teacher
Show me Your way
Lead us in Your way and we
Will follow You all the days of our lives
God, You, are our Teacher
Guide us and train us to go Your way
So that we may follow You
God, You, are our Teacher
Help us to show your way to others
And, when we speak, help us to speak as You want, not our way
God, You, are our Teacher.
We praise You, and only You,
And we will continue to praise You in this life as well as in Your presence

2/16/15

BARNEY

A pet smiles when it is happy,
With its owner.
My dog smiled at me
He protected me
When I was scared
He comforted me
When I was sad and lonely

My dog was my
Best friend
In good times and in bad
We were there
For each other
His name was
Barney

7/3/16

WARRIOR

A warrior is a fighter
If fought
But
With the torment
In my mind
I feel like giving up
I want to get free
To be with Jesus
Is my plea

A warrior is a fighter
How can I fight
When I feel like a coward
To go on
The hurts,
The voices.
Only Jesus can free
Only Jesus can wipe away
Every pain,
Sorrow and tear I cry
I long to be with Him

7/3/16

TRICKLE OF LIGHT

A trickle of light passed
Through my window
Last night

A ray of hope?
I do not know.

The voices were not as bad
And my thoughts slowed down
But

There is a lot of pain
In my life
And
I want to die
To be with Jesus
My only true home
With no more pain,
Sorrow,
Or
Tears.

7/4/16

A PURPOSE

Does God have a purpose
For us?
I used to think so
But
Not any more
I have always been different
From others
I have a lot of pain.

My mind is tormented.
I cry out to God
It is all my fault
Take me
Because I am tired of this
Crying and pain

Does God have a purpose
For us
If He does
Please save me

7/4/16

THE FOG

I woke up this morning
In a thick
Fog enveloping me

Cutting me like a knife
Are my thoughts and memories
All the pain tearing me apart
Its unbearable.
What can is do?

Its eating me alive
Like termites eat wood

I am dying inside
With no way to get free

7/5/16

WHOOPIE PIES

Whoopee pies
What do they do
For me
They help me feel good
When I eat them
They make me happy

There are many different
Kinds
Chocolate peanut butter,
Red velvet,
Lemon,
Oatmeal,
And
Chocolate chip.

They are all good
Eat them,
You cannot go wrong
The best part is the
Cream in the middle

7/5/16

SUNSETS

Sunsets are majestic
Each sunset is
Unique
Like a painting on the sky.
It is God's painting
For us

Sunsets are majestic
Orange,
Red,
And
Purples too.
God's creative masterpiece
It takes one's breath away

Sunsets are majestic
An act of God
Thank him when you
Look at one.

7/6/16

UNTITLED

I want to kill
Myself
I do not care what people think
It is my life
And
My mind is in turmoil
I just want to get free
To go to Jesus

People look at me
And
Think I look happy
But
They are not in my head
Only I know what goes on

All the pain I carry
I am just sick
And
Tired of it all

7/7/16

DAISY

Flowers are pretty
And nice to
Look at
One flower
Is a
Daisy

They yellow center
Reminds me of the sun
And the white petals
Are clouds

You see,
Even in the midst
Of clouds,
The sun still shines
And that makes me happy
Yes
Daisies make me happy

7/8/16

ROSE

They say that every
Rose
Has its thorn
You see
In the midst of the thorns
You can still bloom brightly
Like a rose.

A rose is a beautiful thing
They smell good too

Roses come in different colors
Each one is
Unique in its beauty
Just like each of us is unique
Next time you look at one
Thank him

7/10/16

BUMPS IN THE ROAD

We all face bumps in
The road
But without them our life is
Meaningless
And
Dull
Persevere and soon
You will feel better and pursue your dreams

We all face bumps in the road
Our mind can trip us
Up
But do not give up cause
Our will is strong
We can accomplish
Anything
We want

Keep on peddling
With head held high
We may even learn
To enjoy the ride.
These bumps in the road

7/12/16

PUZZLE

As a puzzle has
Many pieces
So, our lives have
Many pieces

At first the puzzle
Is chaotic
How our lives tend to be

As we put our
Puzzle piece
By piece together
We need to do this
With our lives

Eventually the puzzle
Comes together
Little by little
The picture becomes
Clearer

No one puzzle is the same
What does yours look like?

As I put my puzzle together
I see a picture of myself with
Tears flowing down my face
From the torment that I am in
I yearn to be free from it all
7/15/16

CLOUDS

Remember as children
We would watch the clouds
In the sky
And
See what they reminded us of

The other day I saw a cloud
That looked like
A dungeon
The one I am in,
And cannot get free

I call out,
But
Feel all alone
And
Scared of the deep
Pain I am in.

7/17/16

SUMMER

Four seasons:
Winter, spring, summer
And
fall
Each season has its
Good points
I like summer

In the summer
It is fun to have
Cookouts,
Camping
And
Other activities too.
Like croquet

To lay down in the sun
Is fun too
What is your favorite season?

7/18/16

SWIMMING

In the summer
When it is hot
Try to find things to do
To cool off.
I like to swim

Swimming is good exercise
And
You could go to a
Pool
Or an
Ocean.
Just watch out for sharks.

7/18/16

UNTITLED

The weather can help us
Feel happy
And
Positive
Or
It can make us feel
Sad
And
Depressed

Sun and clouds,
I like the sunny
Weather
Because
It keeps us warm and without it,
Things would not grow as much
We need both rain and sun
I love sunny day's
Because it lifts
My spirits

7/19/16

EMOTIONS

I have many emotions
It is scary
And
I try to hide
I put on a mask
And
I go somewhere by myself
And
Cry

The tears flow from me
It is all the pain
And
Torment attached to me

I hear its ok to cry
Just let those tears
Flow
Because they can bring forth
A healing that we do not feel

I need to remember
This one thing
That I am not alone

7/20/16

WITHOUT A CARE

The clouds float by
Without a care
In the world
It looks so calm
And
Serene

On the clouds
Are all the pain
And
Torment in my mind
Although they
Are
The storm clouds
And
I am afraid of it

Soon the storm clouds
Burst forth
Like when
I hurt myself
There is a little relief
But
The pain and torment
Are there again

7/28/16

FERRIS WHEEL

I am stuck on a
Ferris wheel
Going round and round
All that is in my mind
Keep spinning

I cannot seem to get free
I am afraid of what
Is inside
The pain and torment
Are keeping me
Stuck on it

I am stuck on a
Ferris wheel
I am scared
How can I slow it down?
Take my hand and help me off

7/30/16

JUMBLED

My mind was
All jumbled up
But now it is getting
Clearer

I used to think
Of
The pain and torment,
But little by little
With help from the staff
I am thinking
Of
Happy things

People are here to
Help you
It is not good to hide
And be in hiding
In the prison of your life

For your own good
Reach out
Do not be afraid
Because one
We can have a whoopee pie
Together

8/1/16

TRAP

Trap
I am stuck in a trap
The jaws are
Squeezing the life
Out of me
And I cannot get free
No matter what

I try to keep breathing
But I am being suffocated
By the pain and torment
In my life
Is there a way out?
I need to get free

8/5/16

SECRETS

Secrets kept inside can
Torment you
You cannot live life
A free life

People tell me that I should
Live for my kids
And
Other family too

But

I feel that I am just
A burden
A load
Too heavy to bear

8/9/16

STRUGGLES OF LIFE

The struggle in my life
Is over my
Mind
How do I gain control over it?

I am defeated by the tormented
Thoughts
And
Voices which vie for attention in my life

My personal Olympics
My ultimate gold
Is
To try to forge on

To gain control
Of the mind
One day at a time

Bronze, silver and gold
Are all winners
Keep your eye on the goal

8/10/16

DANCE

Captivated by the dance
But I do not know
How to dance
It is all foreign to me
They say just let yourself move
To the music
To express yourself

Each one is unique in
The way it is done.

Dance of life
Express yourself
Just let yourself move
To the music
The beat of life
Do not hold back
Do not be bashful,
Just move

8/11/16

NATURE

Out in nature
Out in the woods
The beauty
The tranquility
Serenity

The woods
The trees
The animals
And
Other things too

Nature and beauty
Tranquility.

Sunsets on the lakes
With the swans
Gracefully
Laying there too.
Just be there and enjoy the beauty

8/18/16

UNTITLED

Hot coals, searing pain
Ripping me apart
Bit by bit
Until there is nothing left
The voices
The torment
The pain,
How do I get rid of it?
I do not know

Hot coals, searing pain
Get me some ice
Some relief from the
Voices, the torment
And
The pain
The shackles that
Bind me deep within

8/21/16

UNTITLED

Things go on in my mind
That I cannot explain
And
The voices,
The pain
And the torment
I cannot stand it,
I do not know what to do
But
To write and to talk

I feel like a freak
Like no one understands
And at times like no one cares
But they say they do
The only thing I can do
Is try another day.

8/23/16

GLASS SWAN

A long time ago I had a vision
I was a glass vase
Thrown and shattered
In pieces
Along the ground
Unable to make sense
Of any of it

That night though, I had
A dream.
I saw a beautiful
Glass swan
With no blemishes
Out of it
A perfect piece of glass
On display for all
To see

The moral of the story
Is that some day after
A lot of time maybe
That swan will be
Me a testimony for others

8/27/16

UNTITLED

My skin is crawling
My skin is boiling
Out from under me
I need relief from it
I do not know which way
To go
Which way is up
Any more

The sun is torching me
Searing me straight through the core
Of my being.
I need some water
Some parchment
For my soul
Some relief from the desert I am in.

9/6/16

HAUNTING

The voices haunt me
Like ghosts
On a dark
Haunted night,
Everywhere I turn
They are there
I cannot hide
I cannot get any rest

The voices come
And go like
A song in the night
Always there but sometimes
They are better at times

9/20/16

THE OTHER NIGHT

The other night I
Heard them calling
My name.
So, we talked till the wee hours
Of the morning
Till I fell asleep

It scares me because
They want me to do things
To myself that,
I know I
Should not do

It is just that at times
The voices are so strong
They are scary
They will not leave me alone

9/21/16

DARKNESS

Darkness
There is a darkness
That envelopes my soul
As the voices torment me
Day by day

They bind me
With shackles
I fell I cannot get free
Except to give in to them

When I do get
Some rest
I feel good
But it does not last
Cause the voices
Come back
Even more forever

9/24/16

DANGERFIELD

Dangerfield,
Be careful where
You step
Caution
All meant to keep
Us safe
Right where we are
But.

I have a major malfunction
I do not want to be safe
I want to be with
Jesus
Where I will be the only safe
I know
With no more tears, pain or fears
We will be happy forever more

10/9/16

FALL

Fall-the colors
The reds and oranges
And yellows too.
They all are pretty

Events of the fall
Hay wagon rides,
Cookouts with
Marshmallows and hot chocolate
Too.

Pumpkin carving
And do not forget
Pumpkin pies

Fall is a good season
And
I like it also because
My birthday is then.
I smile

10/10/16

MONSTERS

There are monsters
Vying for different
Parts of me
I cannot make it out
Because it is so confusing
I just try to take one day at a time
It is all I can do.

Just knowing I am
God's
Makes me
Smile
Just knowing
I have a purpose
Keeps me going

10/16/16

STANDING

Here is stand on a
Sunny calm day
In the midst
Of the shallows

As the tide comes
In and out
I just stand
There and watch
Waiting patiently
For a sign from
God
That everything
Will be alright
And
Deep down inside
I know it will

Because God
Is in control
And in that, I can rest

10/18/16

GIVING UP

The voices are so bad
I feel like giving up
I lay in bed
At night
Terrified that
They will hurt me

I want to do it myself
End it all so that
I can go to
Jesus
And
Bear it no more

Because with Jesus
There will be no more
Pain,
Sadness,
Crying
Or
Sorrow

11/12/16

UNTITLED

There is a darkness
A certain darkness
That envelopes me
At times

It is hard to move on
But
Somehow, I always
Find a way to
Bounce back
Especially
As I think about
My kids

They always pull me through
The tough days

11/16/16

URGES

I am having urges
To hurt myself
Make the pain
Go away

No one understands
I want to be near
Those I love
They do not care

People will ask me
What my plan is
But
Do they really think
That I am that stupid
To tell them.
Help me my friend

11/28/16

OUTSIDE

I walked out in the
Cold, windy day
For a brisk walk.

I felt free in a
New way
And
I heard the voice of
God
Say to me
That he got my hand
And
That he will be with me
No matter what

12/1/16

TEARS

The tears are flowing
Form the insults
That come from
The mouths
Of others
I try to hold them
Back
But I cannot

Alone at times like
These are hard
Being so far away
From
Family and friends
But
We need to remember
The good times
And slowly
The tears
Dry
As we are with loved
Ones.

12/17/16

STRUGGLE

The struggle for my mind
Is between
Bad and good

The bad are
The voices
And
The good
Are clear headed day's

Truth be told
I am scared
Many day's
When I wake
I do not like who I am
And
What I have become

1/2/17

LOSS

I feel at a total
Loss of control
I am barely able
To make it
During the day
Because
I fall asleep
When I do not want to
I am afraid I will miss
Something important

I am taking one day
At a time
Is all I can do
I do not want to fail
My kids or anyone
Close to me
All I can suggest
To all who read
My writing,
Is do not try to take on
More than you can handle

1/20/17

UNTITLED

The blood drains form
My head as
They hang me
Upside down

The cut just
Drains freely
So that I can
Have my party
With Jesus

No more tears
No more fears
No more sorrow
We will be with
Jesus in heaven

1/21/17

STRETCHING

They stretch me this way
And
They stretch me that way

I feel like silly putty
Confused
Why can't they leave me?
Alone and just
Guide me gently
No tear me apart

I am content being
Silly putty
If
They do not stretch
Me to far

3/1/17

GOD'S PAINTING

A sunrise is like a painting
God's painting on a brand
New canvas
For a brand-new day
A day of new beginnings

A day of new beginnings
To pick oneself up
After a bad day
A day to start fresh

The sunrise is God's beautiful
Masterpiece
Painted across the sky
God's in charge
Of it all
God is awesome

5/11/17

THE TIDE

Thick as fog that descends from
The sky
Are the voices which perverts
My head

The voices come and go like
The tide of the ocean
Sometimes they are loud like the
Waves, crashing on the beach
Other times they are as quiet
Like a lake on a peaceful day

Thick as fog that descends from
The sky
Are the voices which permeates
My head

Sometimes they are loud like a
Roaring waterfall
Other times they are quiet like
Water in a swimming pool

5/11/17

MOTHER'S DAY

Mothers are nurturing
Mothers are caring
Mothers are loving
And
Mothers stick by you
My mother is great

One day a year we celebrate
Our mothers
And what they mean for us
Mothers are special

Mothers are our protectors
Mothers are defenders
Mothers stick by
You
No matter our age
Even if we may be far apart

Happy Mother's Day to all the
Mothers in the world

5/14/17

DO YOU REMEMBER ME?

I wonder in my heart,
Do you remember me?
The times we spent together
Do you remember me?

I wonder in my heart
During this Mother's Day,
Do you remember me?
You would take me out
For a banana split each year
Do you remember me?

I wonder in my heart
Do you remember me?
You were near
Now your gone
And
It makes me sad
Do you remember me?
Will you remember me?

5/14/17

UNTITLED

Tears flow from my eye's
Because I am scared
Scared for my life
I need to be vigilant

Tears flow from my eye's
Because I am scared
I do not know what to do
I feel like hurting myself

Tears flow from my eye's
Because I am scared.
I need to turn to Jesus
Because He is always with me

Tears flow from my eye's
Because I am scared
Afraid of the future
Afraid of the unknown

I just want to break free
To leave this all behind
Help me

5/14/17

SCARY

Yelling and cursing scares me
It makes me uneasy
And
Afraid
Plus, its disrespecting others
And
My faith

I try to use my coping skills
When it happens
But it is hard because
I shake and get anxious too.

Yelling and cursing scares me
Why do people do that?
I think they do it for a power
And
Control trip
Or maybe because they feel
Inadequate themselves

Yelling and cursing scares me
It makes my chest hurt too.

5/16/17

FORGIVENESS

When we have regrets
Of things we've should have done
It may be hard,
But
We need to forgive ourselves

Forgiveness is hard to do
But the more we hold onto things,
The harder it is to forgive
We must practice self-forgiveness
To experience healing

When others have wronged us
Again, it is important not to hold on.
We must forgive
To bring healing
To us and others

Forgiveness is a hard thing
But
It builds character
And
Makes us stronger in the long run

5/17/17

MY NAME POEM

Bright
Enthusiastic
Nice
Jovial
Active
Musical
Innovative
Neat

5/18/17

BOMBARDED

My head is bombarded
With the chains
That bind me fast
The thoughts that are
In there and
The voices are scary too
Is there any respite
Is there any hope
For me at all
I feel hopeless
And
At a loss

Like a hammer and chisel
That cuts,
The voices cut right through me
I am tired and weary
Tired of fighting the fight
I am beginning to think that
There is no victory for me
I feel hopeless and
At a loss.

5/18/17

BIRD'S SONG

I hear a melody each morning
Coming from the birds
Singing their song
What it is,
I do not know
But
It is sure beautiful

I hear a melody each morning
Coming from the birds
Their song is majestic
God's creation

I hear a melody each morning
Coming from the birds
Their song is wonderful
It brings joy to my ears
God's creation
Manifested each day
New every morning
It sure is beautiful

5/19/17

MY HEART

My heart carries many things
Scars and wounds from
Things that happened to me, like
Abuse, abandonment and rejection
These have caused much pain

My heart carries many things
Love from family and friends
With keeps me going on
No matter what

My heart carries many things
Both good memories and bad ones too
It makes my heart glad when
I dwell upon the good

My heart carries many things
The most cherished one is
The love of Jesus
Because
I know that He is with me
No matter what

5/19/17

UNTITLED

No one knows about him,
His name is Vladimir.
He wants me to hurt myself
Wants me to die
Gives me many plans

Vladimir follows me too
And
Rarely lets me go
I do not know what to do
Because it is scary
And
The real me wants to be happy

With this pen and paper
I write it down
Because
I want him to leave
I need to be rescued
He dresses in black, has long black hair
And
Rarely lets me go
Help me!
Get rid of him following me and speaking to me

5/20/17

WEARING A MASK

I wear a mask.
On the outside of the mask
I appear happy
But
On the inside of the mask
I am scared, lonely and afraid

I wear a mask
Outside of the mask
I try to appear like I have
It all together
But on the inside
I am in turmoil
And
Bound by shackles
Unable to get free

I wear a mask
On the outside
I wear content
But
On the inside
I am anxious and do impulsive things

I wear a mask
I need to trust
And
Heal, so that I can have a normal life

5/22/17

FIRE

A fire is blazing in my mind
Burning out of control
With no relief of any kind
Even though the tears
Come at times
And
Quench the fire
It still smolders
And
The fire blazes again

A fire is burning in my mind
Burning out of control
The voices are bad at times
And
Sometimes they are better

A fire is burning in my mind
Burning out of control
I feel like I am all alone
Like no one understands
There are ae thoughts in my mind too
Such evil things I would like to do
Just to end it all
For some relief
What if?

A fire is burning in my mind
Burning out of control
I need to break free
Someday will come and,
I will have my way
And
No one will be able to stop me

5/23/17

COMMITMENT

Commitment is keeping our word
At something
They ask me if I can
Commit to being safe
I tell them yes, but
Inwardly I know I cannot
I am not in that position yet.

Commitment is a sacred thing
One day I would like to
Commit to being safe, but
It will take a lot of work
With people I trust
And
Even work on my part too
Now though, I cannot

Commitment, what is it?
Sticking with something
Even though it may be hard
I cannot do it now
But maybe someday I can

5/23/17

RAINDROPS LIKE TEARS

The raindrops that fall
From the sky
Are like the tears
That fall from my eyes

They are raindrops of
Anxiety, voices and the
Thoughts that race
Through my mind

They are raindrops for
The pain I feel
And
The shackles that bind me
They are raindrops for
Healing; because both
Raindrops and tears bring
Growth and healing to a soul

The raindrops that fall
From the sky
Are like tears that
Flow from my eyes

5/26/17

MIRROR

I look in the mirror
And I see a
Scared, hurting and
Lonely individual
The reflection of someone
That I do not like
With low self-esteem

I look in the mirror
And I see a
Someone that I do not recognize or
Even have compassion for

I look in the mirror
And what do I want to see?
I want to see a
Normal person
Who has good self-esteem?
An individual who is healing
Little by little
Taking one day at a time

5/28/17

BLESSED

I am blessed to have
You in my life
When I am down,
You are my rock
You took me in when I
Was sick
And
Still you stand by me

I am blessed to have
You in my life
You are strong when
I am weak
I am blessed
And
I admire you for
Standing by my side no matter what

I am blessed to have
You in my life
I cherish you and your family
And am blessed
To be a part of your life

6/1/17

SURVIVOR

I am a survivor,
I have survived many things
Like the pain in my life
I am a survivor
I can live through anything
Make it through the toughest day

I am a survivor
I have survived this illness
And the
Tormenting voices
I am a survivor
I can make it through anything
I set my mind to

I am a survivor
I need to make it for my kids
I can do it
I am a survivor
And
Can make it through the toughest day

6/1/17

ALONE

Lord, I feel all alone
I feel like you have
Abandoned me
And
Left me in a dark pit
Just to decay and die

Lord, I feel all alone
I feel stuck with
No way to get out
Like there is no escape
To safety

Lord, I feel all alone
Where ae you?
I cry,
I am tired of this,
Tired of this mess

Lord, I feel all alone
I cannot talk to anyone
Cause I feel like they
Do not understand
Where are you?

6/2/17

SNOWY BLIZZARD

Like a snowy blizzard winter day
My mind goes a mile a minute
The thoughts just keep coming
I can find no rest
No shelter whatsoever to
Protect me

As the snow falls on a winter day
And it is cold outside
I shiver at the things that
Are in my mind
I need to break free
From them
I need protection

Like a snowy blizzard winter day
I am stuck out in the middle of it
Vulnerable to the voices and thoughts
Inside my mind
I am desperate to get some freedom

6/6/17

UNTITLED

When I am with my kids
And talk to them
I feel happy

When I am apart from
My kids,
I feel sad and lonely

When there is chaos
Around me
I feel confused

When I listen to music
And
Do my writing
I feel peaceful

I have trouble pinpointing
Just one emotion,
But,
If I had to pick one it would
Be happy because I am
Around my family and friends

6/7/17

FLOWERS

Flowers, there are
Many kinds
Each of them unique
Like each and every person

One of my favorites is
A sunflower
A sunflower has the center
And coming outward are the
Yellow petals,
Like rays of sunshine
Beaming down on earth

I believe sunflowers are like
The warmth of the sun
Warming the people as they
Look at them
You cannot help but smile

Flowers are indeed pretty
The sunflower is
One of them

6/8/17

UNTITLED

As the tide from the ocean
Washes up seashells
On the beach,
The thoughts enter my mind
At free will

Each time more thoughts wash up
In my mind
And
The voices come and go
They disturb me
And
I feel helpless.
I need rescued

As the tide washes up the shells
The thoughts and voices enter my mind
I try my best to ignore them
But,
They are strong and loud
That it is hard to drown them out

I cry out
Help me, I want to get rid of them

6/14/17

RAINBOW

Beyond the rainbow
There is hope
A hope for a
Better tomorrow and day's ahead

The rainbow is a reminder of
God's promise
A promise that will last forever
God never fails

Beyond the rainbow
There is hope
A hope that is eternal
A hope that will not pass away

A rainbow,
A multitude of colors
Like a painting on the sky
Is a picture of hope
Hope for me
Taking one day at a time

6/15/17

WANTING FREEDOM

I am restless
I want my freedom
To get out of this prison
I am in
I feel stuck
With no way to get out

I am restless
Eager to move on
And
Soar in the sky
I want my freedom
To get out of this prison
I am in

I am restless
Itching to try anew
No more living in the past
Looking forward to the future
I want my freedom
To get out of this prison
I am in

6/16/17

BATTLE

I battle it every day
The thoughts of suicide
And
Hearing the voices
Sometimes they are less
And
Sometimes they are more

I battle it every day
The thoughts of suicide are strong
I try to talk back
To dispel them
But
They will not leave me alone
The voices too.

When will I ever feel better?
When will they go away for good?

I battle them every day
The suicidal thoughts and the voices
What am I to do?
Where can I go for safety

7/9/17

INDEPENDENCE DAY

Independence Day
The men and women
Who fought for our country
We celebrate our freedom
That we are Americans

Independence Day
Cookouts with
Hot dogs, hamburgers,
Potato salad
As well as other goodies
We celebrate our freedom
With family and friends

Independence Day
Fireworks a display
Out of this world
A day we celebrate
Our freedom
The men and women who fought for
Our country

Independence Day
Freedom-we are Americans

7/10/17

ROAD OF LIFE

This road of life is full
Of twists and turns
I have had my share of them
Been locked up for a while
But,
I am ready to take the
Plunge for bigger and better things

This road of life is full
Of twists and turns,
We all have our share of them,
But I have learned a lot,
A lot that I am grateful for:
My ability to write,
Waking up and talking and walking
Family and friends
The list goes on

This road of life is full
Of twists and turns
We all have our share of them

7/11/17

MY SON'S WORLDVIEW

The other night I had
A conversation.
It made me glad
It was with my son
Had a great conversation
It was Fantastic

Each time I shared
Something with him
He would answer with
"That's Fantastic"

What is Fantastic
To him, it is his dreams
And
His pure view of life

The other night I had
A conversation with my son
What is Fantastic for me?
The answer is my blessings:
My kids, and my dreams
And
That I am feeling better
Yes, that is "Fantastic"

7/11/17

UNEASY

When we feel uneasy
In certain situations,
We can get anxious
It can cripple us
Make us afraid to do things

Anxiety comes in many
Different forms
Like: sweating, shaking,
Headaches and upset stomach
There are other symptoms too

Anxiety, what are we
To do when we are afraid?
Sometimes it is best
To take small steps
To ease ourselves in a situation
It can be conquered
Just take one moment
At a time

7/15/17

PERSEVERANCE

When you are feeling down
You persevere
I see a strength that you have
You are working hard to overcome

When you feel weak
Just look where you came from
To be where you are
And
Take one day at a time
With the strength
That you have
I know you will make it
And
Be even stronger in the end

Perseverance is a great quality
Whenever you need it
Just read these words
And
You will make it through anything

7/16/17

THANK YOU

Thank you from the
Bottom of my heart
For helping me
During my dark day's

Thank you from the
Bottom of my heart.
You listened to me when
I would talk

Thank you from the
Bottom of my heart
For guiding me through
The bad day's as well as
The good ones
You all helped me through

I thank you from the
Bottom of my heart
I will never forget you all.

7/17/17

FORGIVENESS

Forgiveness is the battle of
The mind
Especially self-forgiveness
It racks our mind

There are barriers to forgiveness
Guilt is a barrier
Guilt for things that should have been
And
Guilt for things that have been

Forgiveness is essential if
You want to have peace
Both inwardly and outwardly
Forgiveness is a choice of
The mind
One small step toward healing

6/15/17

MY CROSS TO BEAR

This cross feels too much to bear
The voices and the thoughts
Are scary at times
When I feel scared, lonely, sad and depressed
I like to listen to music

This cross feels too much to bear
But I need to rely on people
And coping skills
It is hard I know,
I am not alone

Sometimes I cry,
Sometimes I am in pain
But
The Lord can help me carry my cross

5/2/17

MASK

I wear a mask
Confident, strong, and happy
But, behind the mask
I feel sad, lonely, depressed
And
I hear voices which scares me

I wear a mask
Behind the mask I feel:
Dumb, ugly, and unconfident
With low self-esteem
Wondering why I am here
Wondering why I struggle
With this illness
But
I remind myself
That I have a purpose
Which is to be used by God

5/8/17

FIGHTER

You are a fighter
You have a determination
That infects my soul
A determination to
Make it for my kids

You speak your mind
A determination that
I admire
A determination to keep on keeping on

You are a friend and a good listener too
You are a fighter and a true friend
That I can trust
A word of advice though
Just continue to be you
The fighter that I see
And
You will do great things

5/9/17

FEELING BETTER

I said a prayer for you
Last night
I do not like to see you hurt
Cause your my friend

You are my friend
Your smile is infectious
It brightens up my day
As I give you this blessing

I pray that God will take
Away your pain
That God will heal you this day
Cause you are my friend

You are my friend
You see the good in me
That I cannot see in myself
If there is one lesson, I learn from you,
It is to try to see some good in me

5/10/17

FRIENDS

Friendship is a rare thing
True friends are hard to find
But when you have one
Do not take it for granted

Friends, true friends
Stick by you
They tell you the truth
Even if it may hurt
Cause they got your back

Friends listen to your
Hopes and dreams
Friends even listen when
Your day may be hard

Friends, true friends
Stick by you
No matter the cost
When the going gets rough
Your friend is there.
Thank your friend

5/12/17

PRAYER

Your hurting inside
I can see your pain,
But
I pray to see you smile
To see you happy and
Enjoying the day

Your hurting inside
I see you cry
If I could wipe away your tears
I would do it in a jiffy
Cause I want you to be happy

Your hurting inside
I see your pain
You are my friend and
It makes me sad
To see you that way
But
I will say a prayer for you each day

5/12/17

ALWAYS

I am here and I love
You very much
Even though we may
Be apart at times
I carry you with me
Cause you are my grandchildren
And you are so precious to me

You are my heart and soul
You are close to my heart
And
You will be forever

I look forward to our
Special times together
And
Many more as you grow

I am here and I love you very much

5/12/17

TRUE REST

The voices were bad yesterday
I kept thinking
If only?
If only I could walk
In front of this
Car
Or
That truck.
Then I could go to heaven
And have no more pain
Sadness, crying, or sorrow
Because I will be with Jesus

Jesus is the ultimate
Healer I need
To find my
True rest in Him

4/4/17

BONE CHILLING COLD

A bone chilling coldness
Envelopes me
When I hear the
Voices
It scares me and
Terrifies me
I fear to keep going
Because of
What others might think

I want the voices to
Leave me alone
So, I can be happy
And normal
Not a freak
I somehow need to get rid of these
Feelings and thoughts
What they are telling me
I believe, because
It has been such a long time,
All my life

4/6/17

UNTITLED

Each day that comes I notice
A difference
The voices are getting less
And the urges for self-harm
Have gone down too
I just need to take one
Day
At a time
And
Go to someone I trust
When I do feel bad

I will not feel afraid
because they are my friends

4/7/17

UNTITLED

I like to sit in the
Darkness
Because I do not
Have to
Confront m fears
And the bad things that
Happened to me
In my past

I can just go to sleep
And
Sleep it off
Till the next day,
When it just happens
All over again
Like the merry go round
That it feels like I am on.

4/8/17

STRANGER IN A BIG WORLD

I feel like a stranger
In a big world
Afraid to
Tell
My problems to
Because I do not want
To be a burden

I just want to check out
Because I am being stretched
Too thin like
A ball of silly putty

I feel like a stranger
In a big world
Looking up things
I know I should not
Cause I need to be
Around for my kids

But I am such a big burden
They deserve someone whole
Not broke like me
Who is a stranger in a
Big world

4/13/17

NUMBERED DAY'S

My days are numbered
What will I be remembered by?
My words
Or
My deeds

One day soon I will be
In my home sweet home
Heaven's perfect place

This pain is unbearable
I am a slave to
My mind
Being held captive
By the thoughts deep within

I cry out to a deaf world
It seems,
I feel like nobody hears
Like nobody cares

What should I do?
Where can I go
But to my home
In heaven above.

6/10/16

MASHED POTATOES

Like a bowl of mashed potatoes
My mind feels
All mushed
Together
And I cannot make sense out
Of them

So many things going
On up there
I am afraid of it all
Cause of the pain I feel
I want to get free
From the shackles that
Bind me

I cry out because
Of the
Pain
Just let me be
And
Let me die so that
I can be free.
Cause that is the only way I know to
Get rid of all this pain

6/12/16

SPINNING MIND

My mind spins
Out of control
My thoughts are all
Jumbled up
And make my mind
Hurt

The jumbled mess
Are all memories
Like sand of the beach
There are many
But
There is much pain
I need some rest,
I yearn to get free
But how?

I write and get
Some rest
I talk and get
Some rest too
But
It does not last

In the end I try to
End it all
Cause that is the only
Way I know

To be free indeed
Is to be with Jesus
My Savior and my God

6/14/16

A DARKNESS THAT ENVELOPS ME

Like the darkness at night
There is a darkness that
Envelops my mind
A pain
So deep that I
Find it hard to go on
I just want to give in
To the desire of my soul
And have a
Grand Welcome to Heaven party

No one understands
It seems,
The way I feel
There is a deep darkness
That envelops
My mind

So many hurts and
A pain so deep
That I cry out to all who hear
Please help me, take my hand
And lead me
It all resides in me
It is my choice to do
What I want.
I would be better off dead,
My grand welcome to heaven party

6/17/16

EMPTY

I feel so empty and lost
A life with no purpose
I life in the
Dark

Sometimes I hear them
And it scares me
To no end
I am in turmoil and
I just want it to end
A life lived in the dark
I will die I know,
But then I will be in the light
In Heaven above
With no more pain

I feel so empty
And lost
Why can't I go now?
To be free from it all

6/18/16

ALIENATED

I feel alienated from
My family and friends
Like no one
Understands me
What I have been through
Or
Where I have been

The pain that is
Deep inside me
My mind is in turmoil,
What can I do?

I am and outsider
Looking in
I am afraid of living
Afraid to go on
I want to die
To be free from the pain and voices
That bind me and shackle me
I am in a prison in a dungeon all alone

6/19/16

MIND LIKE A SPONGE

My mind is like a sponge
It soaks in everything
I see and hear
The good and the bad
But the bad outweighs the good
There is much pain
In my mind
It cannot get it out

I have things that are
Good in my life
But I also have a lot of bad
And it scares me

There is much pain
And I do not want to go on
I want to be in Heaven
Where there is no more pain
And where Jesus will wipe away
Every tear I have.

6/19/16

STEALTH

They call me stealth
Cause I am
The
Loudest one,
The most vivid one

There are others
But
I am the source
He hates himself
And
One day he will succeed
He will give himself over
To death of this life

6/20/16

WOUNDED

I look in the mirror
And see
A wounded person
With a pain so deep
That I want to hide.
But I still see it every day

I cry, but it is
Still there
What can I do?
To be free
I want it all to end

I look in the mirror
And see a
Wounded person
With a pain
So deep
It scares me.
I see,
I know,
That only true freedom
From pain is
In Heaven

6/20/16

UNTITLED

They call me wounded
My mind hurts
Is tormented within
By the voices and things
That have happened
To me

I put my guard up
Cause I have been touched
In bad way's at
Places I have gone to for help
Why did that happen
What did I do to deserve it?

6/20/16

"BELLA"

My friend Bella said
She would be there to help
To encourage
To be an ear
But we talked and she yelled
And
Cursed at me which hurt

It is hard to understand
When you are not with the person
But she has a point
I need to find someone I trust to
Tell them my hurts and pains
Please send someone my way.

6/20/16

GOOD AND BAD

In my mind there is good
And
In my mind there is bad
My mind hurts a lot
I just want to
Be dead
How can I fix what is
Broke

What can lift me up?
My kids
But
I think they would be better off
If I was dead

One thing that brings me hope
Is God's word which
Sheds light on
What is broke
How can I fix it?
What can I do?
I just want to get rid of this pain in my mind
A haunting of the devil
And
His schemes and vices too

What can I do?
Where can I go to escape the pain
I try, I cry,
But to no avail
Till something works
And I am with Jesus forever more.

5/17/16

QUIET ASSASSIN

A quiet assassin
Lives inside me
Coming to life at
Any moment

The quiet assassin wants
To see me
Dead
And thrives when I
Take pills
To drown my pain

A quiet assassin lives
Inside me,
Sleeps,
But awakens at any moment
The quiet assassin loves
To see me hurt inside
And keep silent to those around me

The quiet assassin lives
Inside me.
What can I do to escape it?
To get free from the quiet assassin

5/18/16

UNTITLED

In each of us there
Is a demon
Vying for the parts of us
No one can touch
Trying to ruin us

In each of us there is an angel
Changing us from the
Inside out

In each of us there is
A good and a bad
Molding us for the bad
If we allow it
Or
For the good
But we must allow it

So therefore, my charge
Is allow for the good
The angel
To shape us for the good
And not for the bad

5/19/16

HEAVY

My heart is heavy
Upon me
Like a boulder
Being pulled down
Through the Center of my being

My heart is heavy
Upon me
I wish I could just
Give up and give in
To the desires of my life

My mind is heavy
Upon me
It all I can do to keep
Going on
And Not giving up

My heart is heavy
Upon me
Like a boulder
Being pulled through the center of my being
I cry out in agony

Can anybody hear me,
Does anybody care
Come take my hand and lead me
to a place of rest

5/19/16

A SWARM OF BEES

As a swarm of bees
Buzz around my head
So, go my thoughts
A million miles a second

They make my
Mind hurt
Cause I cannot stop them
Do not know how to let them go and just be

They fester till I act on them and
End up hurting myself
I just want to end the pain I feel
And be free from the torment in my mind

I try to talk about it, to lessen the pain
I try to write about it
But still it festers
I become fixated on the thoughts
Till I act and end up regretting what I did

The thoughts attack my mind
I talk sometimes and they still hurt me
I pray for a way out
For someone to come and ease the pain
Rescue me please
Help me find a way out

5/21/16

GRANDPA

Grandpa,
I miss you.
I miss our times together
Just conversating
And
Spending time together

Grandpa
I wish I could be in
Heaven with you

Grandpa
I miss you
Every day it is hard to go on
Without you
I wish I could be with you
In Jesus presence

Grandpa
I miss you
Please say a prayer for me
That ill have the strength
To go on
Till Jesus calls me home
Oh, what a day that will be
When I have my
"Welcome to Heaven" party

5/24/16

THE THUD

Thud, thud, thud
Goes my thoughts
Round and round
Like a fan
It makes my mind hurt
Pain deep within

I cannot control them
Do not know how to
Let them go
And
Just be
It is so hard to do

I have secrets that
I am scared to reveal
Plans that just need to stay
A mystery, or I risk
People judging me
Assuming things
That might hurt me

5/26/16

UNTITLED

Every day is the same
How are you?
They ask
I say fine
To get them off my back
But inside me resides much pain

I want to feel better
I want to be free
I cry out for a hand
To guide me
To a kind of rest
Where no one can harm me

I want to be open but,
I am scared
Of what people may think

Every day is the same
People ask how I am doing
I am fine, I say to get
Them off my back

5/27/16

MARATHON

My mind races as though
It was in a marathon
There is no rest for the
Weary
It seems so crazy
It just keeps on going

I have things in my mind
I am afraid of
I want to run and hide
Because I am scared
Of what is inside

My mind races
I just want to do it and get
It over with
I will be in heaven anyway one day
With those I love

Just stop the race,
I am on the loosing team
But my mind keeps on going

5/28/16

POP CORN

Popcorn is good
In many settings
Movies,
Play's
Concerts too

There are different varieties
Of pop corn
Jalapeno,
Garlic,
Butter and
Carmel too

Pop corn
I like it if it
Does not get stuck in my teeth
How about you?
What kind do you like?

5/28/16

Made in the USA
Middletown, DE
15 September 2021